Nerrissa Jenkins

Published by ISELFEXPRESS
Copyright © 2014 by Nerrissa

Edited by Latasha Snell, Katisha Bennett and Darryl Rivers
Front and Back Cover: The Infinity Media
Author Photo by Nerrissa Jenkins

Website: www.ISELFEXPRESS.com
Email: nerrissa2406@hotmail.com

Manufactured in the United States of America

ISBN-13: 978-0615938974

Dedications

Thank you God for the many blessings.

My siblings and the best friends a sister could ever have
Dermarc, Telyna and Farrah
You are my rocks and my pillows,
It is because of you this journey has been possible.

To my adorable children
Jasmine, Joey and Ryan,
you are my reason for living.

To my Dad, although your time here was short the memory of
your love will live forever...

and to one of the greatest women I have ever known...

My Mother

My *M*other, oh my God
This woman was extraordinary
The woman who gave birth to me
The woman who took care of thee

My *M*other
This woman was extraordinary
A loving mother
One who always supported and helped others
She would give what she had
To bring people out of their struggles

Oh my God
This woman was extraordinary
Had her own style
She did not walk a straight path
She loved my father
Although he whipped her ass

This woman was extraordinary
She kept a roof over her children's head
Made sure we were fed
Although she had her many addictions that never stopped her
She handled her business
She got all that the welfare could give us

This woman was extraordinary
Over the years her choices made her ill
HIV, Dialysis and Drugs
Although she faced those challenges
She sustained
Who she was
My *M*other
Extraordinary!

R.I.P Vanessa R. Turner (My mother)
10/16/52 – 09/17/96

5

Content

Chapter 1: A Divine Interruption

Chapter 2: Just Amazing

Chapter 3: From Me to You

"*Under every hood, is a mysterious women.*"

Nerrissa J.

A
Divine
Interruption

Why I Write

I write because I'm sad

I write because I'm glad

I write because this is what I like to do

Writing unwinds me

It gives me power

It helps my soul

And stimulates my brain so I'm in control

Writing gives me a chance to think

Writing and listening to tunes

Relaxes my mind

And allows my words to come out

Why I write?

To share my story and let the world know

Everybody goes through something

Happy days

Sad days

Good days

Bad days

Rainy days

Snowy days

Days that are just okay

I write because it's real stuff, from the heart

I write because this is who I am

Nerrissa

A single mother

A degree earner

A spaghetti strainer

I'm one woman that conquered all but has failed none.

R & B

If I were

R&B

I would be smooth

When you close your eyes

I would make you move

I would ease your mind

I would give you something to think about

I would relax your soul

And make you float

Sweep you off your feet

I would give you strength

Show who you are

Make you feel good

I am *R*ich & *B*lack

Dance for Me!

My very first piece (2004)

CHANGE HAS COME

Change has come.
Those words I never thought I would be able to say.
I see the impact Barack Obama has left us today.
He isn't just our first African American president,
he is a man who made Dr. King's dream come true.
Obama has touched this world; what more could we ask him
to do?
To see is to believe and know that you could do anything!
Whoever thought this day would come?
After all the hard work Martin Luther King Jr. has done.
From slavery to presidency is what we experienced.
Now it's time for us all to enjoy this very special moment.
For so long we have been divided by color, we were called
inferior.
"I have a dream" is what Dr. King told us.
"This is our time" is what Barack Obama worked for.
This remaking of America is what we've all been waiting to
see,
it's a huge change for our communities.
"Hope for a glorious beginning,"
"No more tears" and
"A nation ready to see history."
The lynching's, the running, the beatings and torturing is
what our ancestors went through; working for the white
man is all they knew.
Yes, "Change has come,"
When my two year old daughter can identify Barack Obama,
I know change has come.
Let's join together and work to change the morale in this
world,
We fought long and hard to get where we are today.
Let by gones be by gones and start a new day.
Our issues and problems aren't enough to hold grudges,
let's come together and be thankful for each other.

Heartless

Heartless Man wonders why
You're not thoughtful, nice or even fly
But when I express my feelings
He thinks I'm complaining all the time
I tell him
It's the pain in my heart
The hurt inside
It's the look in my eyes
All of these emotions are trapped inside
Heartless Man,
That's who you are....

I started to clean
To cool myself down
I'm thinking why, why this man
As stubborn as he is with his selfish ways,
Who would he want to stay?
Is it the passiveness in my personality?
And my high tolerance level?
The decisions I make
And what I sacrifice for others?
Heartless man,
That's who you are....

He can't understand
My strong ways
That's because he never dealt with
A real woman
My strength is huge
It's those beatings I saw
The cocaine vials I found
The molestation I went through
The deaths I experienced
Heartless Man

That's you

I tell him
My story over and over
I can't understand why he doesn't get it
It's the experiences I've gone through
And the knowledge I've gained
The degree I earned
The career I've claimed
Heartless Man
That's who you are....

The Victim

I thought I was safe all the while I was being raped

By my parents who abandon me

Home with my siblings was where I was supposed to be

Suffering from sleepless nights

Scared to close my eyes and holding every part of my body

real tight....

Laying in another stranger's bed

Thinking to myself about what I just did

The cycle just repeats itself

I was a victim of abuse

Now I'm the abuser

I said to myself

Oh my god

What did I just do

This is learned

I did what I knew

Time and time again I made an excuse

It is time,

I get help and check out my mental health.

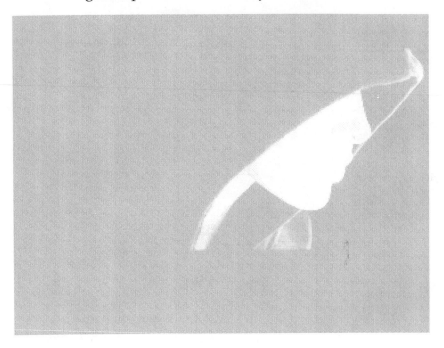

"Hotel"

Residents, who are they?

They are people,

"Homeless"

Is that what they came to be?

Drugs, alcohol and sex

Is that what lead to the devastation?

Their physical being and thoughts

Had no control of the situation

How, how could this be

The drugs, alcohol and sex

Was it used for pain and pleasures?

Their needs and wants were everything

Their homes, their children, their goals…

Pipe dreams!

Why, how could this be from the pain and pleasures?

No support is how the homeless came to be…

He Saved Me

Alcohol became my

Breakfast, lunch and dinner

I can remember so clear

When I took my first sip

Didn't really like the way it made me feel

I said

I was going to quit

But then I lost my job

Then my wife

Before I looked up

I was homeless

I had no idea what was going on

I went from having everything

To pan-handling

In the blink of an eye

My life changed

I had to figure out

Something before I

Ended up in a grave

From being on a street corner

Doing what I do.

An old friend called my name

And said

What happened to you?

I looked up

Lost for words

It was my buddy who I grew up with

He said to me

"Your life doesn't have to be this way."

I know of a program,

If you're willing to stay...

An angel dropped down on me

Lifted my spirits

And said

You can do this

From that day forward

I decided to get clean

It's been 12 months

AA has become

My breakfast, lunch and dinner

My next journey in life

Is to get back what I lost

My job and my wife....

She Beat The Odds

Only 16 with a life in the wound

Her mother said,

"If you're going to be with him, why don't you wait?"

Her conscience

Told her …

Keep the baby

The thought of murder

Not a maybe

At 16 she didn't worry about how things would be

She was confident in her decision making

She was going to raise her child and succeed

Now, years later

Although she was young

Her daughter is in college

It was about the parent she'd become

In fact, not one but three to focus on,

With experience

She said to herself

"I beat the odds"

Life happens

We grow and learn what's important,

Anything is possible

HARD HEADED

Right now I don't know

How to feel

I have a nephew

Who's going to jail

His mom sacrificed

So many things for him

That is what I'm talking about

Ungrateful youth!

Today's children don't have to work hard for anything

The parents we are today,

Because some of us lived a certain way

We try to protect our children from everything...

This is not the way to raise children!

We have to put our foot down and

Teach them nothing is going to be easy

It angers me that my nephew

Is going to jail

He isn't a thug

He walked around here with

His pants below his butt

He walked around pretending to be tough

But when he became cuffed

He was calling all of us

I'm saying this to say

Listen, watch and pay attention

To what your parents tell you today

Jail and death are not the only two ways!

Taken

I thought it was you

I wanted and needed

Confused maybe

Blinded

You told me and you showed me

Who you are

Arrogant, Vengeful, Controlling, Selfish and Uncaring

I should have believed you

Taken…

By lust

A clogged brain

Disoriented thoughts

Trying to make sense of what was the obvious

Confused, maybe

I thought It was you

I wanted and needed

Who was I?

Arrogant, Vengeful, Controlling, Selfish and Uncaring

I should have believed in me

Allowing you to run over me

You never told me you loved me

or made it special for me without agony

Our pre-conceived thoughts

Its because

of "We"

we earned our degree

its because

of "We"

We are who

We are

"We"

Made Us!

A Cruise Shipmen

They're on different cruises 6 months at a time
Did you ever think
How they live their lives
Leaving their families at home
Working day in and day out
Just to provide
Wow
They really have it tough
The nature of their positions
Are wearing many hats
They go from
Room service
Waitressing
Cleaning
And being polite to every guest
Their job is like no other
They work harder than the average person
Us cruisers should be grateful for these shipmen
Our time there is well spent
All the while they're showing us a good time
Their families are home alone,
Waiting for them to arrive.

Fitness Became Me

Discipline

Of my mind

A plan

To move forward

Motivated

Strength

Dedication

Focused on my dream

Spiritual health I crave

Evaluated

Results

Pushing everyday

It is a hell of a lot of work

No rest for the weary

But nourished

Knowledge became my water when I was thirsty

Self-awareness became my vitamin

Rebirth

Freedom

Fitness

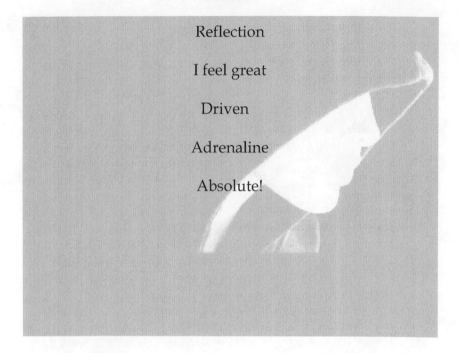

Reflection

I feel great

Driven

Adrenaline

Absolute!

The Academy

The Academy

Up at 5am

Working out everyday

Is not what I expected

After seeing so much despair

Experience opened my eyes

Run, Jump, hurdles

Defined

If I had to change my mind

I would not change it for the world

Discipline

A rare commodity

Get into it

Halt!

Deal with it

Quitting is not an option

Dream…

Deferred…no!

I wanted

Stress and pressure

Never discouraged

My life could change

Just being

A mother, wife, sister, daughter and officer

The Academy

Was all I knew

Broken...remolded

In time

We would be done

The end

Gratitude

The Academy

Survival

Strive to preserve life

Respect, honor and loyalty

All that we should be

"but"

Corruption like a cancer

Can destroy

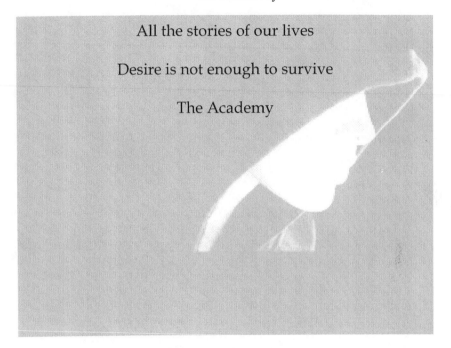

All the stories of our lives

Desire is not enough to survive

The Academy

Inspired by The Police Academy

Class of 7/2005

Enforce

Here is what it's all about
Stopped...frisked
For nothing
Fourth amendment
Damn!
Really
Suspicion
Me or you?
Reasonable doubt
They do whatever they want
We do whatever they say
Cornel West
Review, Analyze, evaluate
Stop & frisk, riot the risk
Terry vs. Ohio
US vs. U.S.
Affected
Color of the skin
Our son
Our brother
Our uncle
Our father
Shit
Even our grandfather
Unite
Take a stand for our rights
To prevent needless loss of life

Little me

I put my shoes on the wrong feet

My hand on my hip

I entered the classroom and said is this it

Tables and chairs just my size

Letters from A to Z

Numbers oh boy 123

Little Me

I'm wondering what this will be

I can only imagine, envision what I see

Dogs, Cats, Lions and Bears

It was just that puzzle I found over there

Wow, they all have a lot of hair

Little me

After a long days work

I grabbed my book bag and said let's go

See you later my teachers

Tomorrow will be a new day!

Born A Boy

The baby of 4
The only boy
For some reason
I loved to play dress up
I never felt confused
About my feelings
I loved to steal
My sister's lip stick and
Put it on my lips
I wanted so bad to grow up
To develop tits and hips
I had no clue of how
That would come true...
It was my dream
It was the feeling I had inside
I wanted long hair
I would sneak in my grandmother's room
And pick one of her wigs
My imagination of becoming
This beautiful girl was so real
My siblings never put too much energy
Into how I felt
But that day I became of age
My family looked at me as if they saw a ghost
I said to them
I was just BORN a Boy
The revealing of who I am was out
I knew no matter how any of them felt
I was the one who had to live and deal with it

Fatherless Girls

What I see is me
Losing my father at 14
I always wondered how things would be
Only if my father was here to see
That I be the mother of 3?

Fatherless girls
What do they have to look forward to
So many girls have no clue
Some become prostitutes
Many become drug users, homeless,
Subjects of domestic violence, suitable to nonsense and losing
everything they got

Fatherless girls
They grow up seeing the obvious
A man that is not their father
A man that never becomes their husband
A man that has no good intensions for them
A man that just wants to take advantage of them
A man that will introduce them to drugs
A man that would even sell his own kids

Fatherless girls
They suffer at times from not having a father
Fatherless girls are searching for love in all the wrong places
Not having a father isn't always negative
Some of the best individuals come from single parent
households
Fatherless girls could be looked at as a stigma
But not having a father is what you make of it.
Fatherless girls

The Unspoken Words

Together for twenty years
Married half the time
A perfect family it seems
Him, baby daughter and me

Reminiscing
About the way things use to be
Verbally abused, mentally confused,
Battered like a slave

Something in my mind
Told me to stay
Not knowing what my life would be
After the abortions, miscarriages
And the operations
I did not know what to think
Or who to call

My mother told me I'm stubborn
And one day I would fall
At that time I stood tall
Disobeyed my mother's orders
I was at my worst

I was afraid to call her
Although she told me this
I knew if she found out from someone else
She would be pissed
So, I got off my high horse,
Called my mother to rescue me
She came running like I knew she would
Pressed my husband to the wall

From that day forward
I honored my mother's words

Remaining faithful in my marriage
Therapy worked

Our beliefs and faith in GOD
Kept our union holy

My Space

Too many people
Read a person through the eyes of social media
How could you
I am not my Avatar
It's baffling how
Individuals perceive others
Clean out your own inbox
No need to judge
You will never understand another's baggage
Advice to the wise…and the fool
Know your own skin
Never build a dream off of another's
You will only wake up in a nightmare
No two minds are alike
You can only accomplish that which you are
Understand
Anyone can think
But only a few can do

Tearful

It's that feeling inside
The tears in my eyes
My vision blurred
My emotions released
I thought of what just happen to me
A slap across my face
A feeling of disgrace
Everything went black
Holding our baby girl, real, real tight
My eyes were opened
This nigga done lost his mind
Flashbacks of a childhood gone by
The one thing not allowed
Abuse
My reaction
Protect my baby
Then things really got crazy
I was in a mood that wasn't becoming
Hell
Why am I going through this
Once, twice, three times too many
Think of a child hopping around
I'm pounding on this nigga
Heads and broom sticks now
Running from my rage
He's afraid to come out
The fire in my eyes, I see him in the flames
He'll think before he strikes
Never again placing his hands on my life

<u>She Whispers</u>

I was so angry

I felt like I was on fire

My insides were burning

It almost felt like an animal eating at my flesh

The feeling I could not suppress

I needed to let go

But never been put in this situation before

It was new to me

The thought of change was overwhelming for me

It was so much to think about

How I would move on

It was difficult to shake this pressure

Although I knew

It was for the better

I had a knot in my chest

I wanted somebody, anybody

To tell me this is it

My moment, my chance

To be free

Unwind

And

Release the demons in me

I was so angry

I soon realized

This too shall pass me!

Infliction

The answer was no

I refused to listen cooked dinner

I told him to come get it

There was no change in his answer

I went shopping;

I spent rent money on new

Underwear

Socks

Shirts

Pants

Sneakers

All for him

But still

The answer was no

I went to his block

Where he normally was

He saw me and acted like I did not exist

I showed up at a birthday party for him

Mingled with his friends

I sent flowers, cards, edible arrangements

Just because...

I put cars and apartments in my name

The answer was still the same

The phone rang at 3am

"Open the door"

He said

They were standing there him and her

I let them in

We did our thing

Months went by the answer was still the same

I got very sick; it was time to go

Hospitalized for a month

Diagnosed with HIV

Why do we....

Ever had a motive?
Wanted to conquer someone....
Were very forceful....
Had low self-esteem....
Obsessed with the person....

Why do we?....
Its because you lead me....
Its because you told me....
Its because you made love to me....
Its because you took me home....
Its because I drove your car....
Its because you were kind to me....
Its because you showed me you can care....
Its because I had your child....

Why do we?....
We do because of Mental Health reasons....
We do because we think we're in love....
We do because they gave us money....
We do because they took our virginity...
We do because they made love to us....
We do because they said "I love you"....
We do because they said you're the only one....
We do because they gave us keys to the house....
We do because they brought us a car....
We do because they met our family....
We do because they exploited us....
We do because we were good enough to have their child....
We do because we can be crazy as hell....
We do because we can be damn fools....

See What

See what is in your face

Don't believe everything

He or she says

Actions speaks

Louder than words

You might think

This is the person for you

No, wake up and realize

Your being boo boo the fool

See what is in your face

Watch their routines

Don't believe everything

He or she says

The excuse about being busy

Never being able to spend time with me

See what is in your face

Communication

via text

stop being a pawn to the

bullshit

Have you ever looked into the mirror?

What did you see?

A beautiful individual like me.

See what is in your face

He or she is lying about

The relationship

Love

Is not suppose to hurt

When it does

Its time for you

To wake the fuck up

See what is in your face

Things you think are good

Turn out to be a disgrace

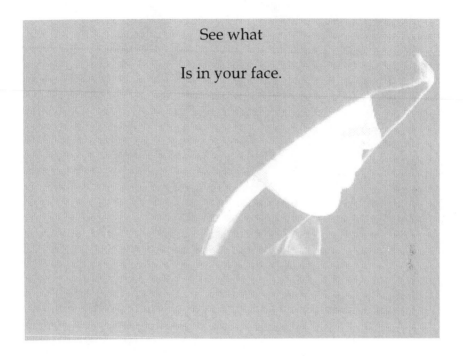

Down

Feeling like there's no support

All alone

In a place not like home

Walls closing in

There are no sounds

Standing in the middle

Watching the world go round

Down, down is the word

Expressions, depressing and feeling by yourself

You stop,

You think,

You say it's only a dream...

Down

Our Struggles

My mom needs rent

"I have to succeed and do this"

No privileges

Do you remember our conversation?

Well, I do

Back in the day

Our parents struggled

Our goals is to work hard

And not be like our parents

But... some of us got caught up

Arrested development,

Having kids, getting high and selling drugs

Some can identify with what's important

Today our youth focuses on the now

Life in the fast lane,

Today's parents

Want to be friends with their children

Instead of being the role models that they need

There is more to life than just trends

Fame,

Popularity,

Fast money

Are not the only ways to achieve success

Responsibility is good for growth!

Expired

I'm not supposed to rehash the past

Those words that struck every part of my brain

It was like the sound of thunder,

Nature, no control over the pain

Lying on the operating table open heart surgery

Never showing any signs of anything being wrong

moving forward

But never forgetting the past is how I got through

Weakness became my strength

Determination

Discipline

Structure

Was how I would make it

Life

Is what I remember

Thanking God for giving me another chance

Forget never, growth and healing forever!

JUST
AMAZING

Satisfaction

It's pleasure that a man gives
It's passion that a women feel's
The intimacy the two have
It's that good loving going in my ass
Oh... those gentle touches from his strong hands
Rubbing on my back such smooth skin
The strokes going in and out
The screams that come out my mouth
It seem like a dream
He's pulling my hair like tug of war
Moving much faster asking if I want more
Oh keep going do not stop
This is the best cock I have ever got
Who would have ever known he could hit the spot
Slowly he pulls it out
He tells me to lie on my back
His body is on top of me
My pussy is tender and moist
He opens his mouth and pulls his tongue out
My clit is hard as a rock
He attaches his wet lips to my clitoris
And start to do his thing
My mouth opens and I start to suck the shit out of his penis
We're in the groove
We're both moaning
Enjoying this 69 position
It was like a video being played
Our bodies are both being laid
Music is playing low
Our movement started to flow
And before you know
Our brains explode
It was awesome, it was great
That was one of the best sex tapes made
Satisfaction...again

Horny

The wetness
The warmest
Can you really handle this?
The feeling and all the sexual healing
Are you able to deal with it?
The juices "Look"
Brings a smile to my face
Is it real or is it fake
You stop,
You think.
You say
For god sake
Is it real or is it fake
How long can you take it?
The pleasures not thinking
About the measures you try
To enjoy it and forget about
The consequences
Is it real
Is it fake
How can you deal with this
Horniness

Just Call Him Bobby

He sticks to the wall
He sticks to the door
He even sticks to the floor
When I'm alone and I feel a way
I pull Bobby out of the draw
He always saves the day
I bounce up and down on him
If I'm just that freaky
I might suck it, jerk it, jump on it and fuck it
It's just the size for me
I keep him near
I never know when
I'm going to need him again
Yeah
I said his name is Bobby
He does the job when I'm alone I use him to solve the problem

Lips

As I sat in the chair awaiting my turn

Finally it was time.

Oh my,

The thoughts that raced through my mind.

I always knew how my admirers viewed my lips.

Now,

this time,

The world gets to see them.

The mysterious me will soon be revealed

And all the words you will now hear;

The smooth,

Luscious,

Sexy,

Kissable,

Great,

Alluring,

Happiness,

And most importantly, the juicy lips!

Give it Up

Oh my

It's gushing out

Like a water fall

She closed her eyes

As he crept up her walls

She reached below him

To massage his balls

The thought that ran through

Both their minds

The nerves in their bodies

Started to tingle one at a time

He maneuvered his tongue

Up the crevice of her ram

All the while the other sucked

On her clitoris

Oh my (Two)

Things just got wild

It was her turn to

Show out

She took the palm of her hand

Wrapped it around his penis

She salivated all over it

Bent up in the air

While the other worked

His way in

Her hands glided

like putting on lotion

up and down her legs

it was warm

it was swollen

before she knew it

both her lips

were wide open

Boom!

There she goes

Deep throating all of it

Oh my

She sucked it out

Until his body went limp

Finally she stopped

"Now"

That's how

You ladies

Should always take control of them!

FROM ME TO YOU

Gone "but" Never Forgotten

There was music, conversation and laughter

Of course it was

There was a party

The phone rang

It was my cousin

Saying

My baby brother was shot with a gun

All I could remember is my body going numb

He was only 14

On the honor roll

and two basketball teams

We knew for sure

He would be a player like Lebron James

Brain dead is what the doctor said

I couldn't believe what was told to me

I wondered if it was a dream

Senseless death

Because of jealousy and envy

My brother lost his life due to a cocksucker

His death, an accident

How could it be?

When an individual pointed at him intentionally

The system failed us again

Now

My baby brother

Is in HEAVEN

RIP Xavier Daniel Jenkins

03/04/1986 to 04/21/2002

BIG BROTHER

He had love for his

3 sisters

Like no other...

The sacrifices he made

Putting food on the table

He'd always been a stand up dude

He never was a hustler like some of these fools

He was always a real big brother

Making sure these fellas

weren't trying to get over on his sisters,

That they made sure to choose decent men

Because their big brother's opinion was important to them

A big brother's role is what he played

And till this day, his 3 sisters' hearts stay the same.

Inspired by our big brother Dermarc aka Dink

He's the designer

He has the sketch to create
The style to want
He is that dude
He is so freaking hot
He has the attitude that will make you lose your mind
He has that walk that makes him so damn fine
He knows how to dress you
As well as caress your brains
You'll think, you just got laid
His qualities are unique
He'll have you saying maybe
Just maybe...
You'll think to yourself am I going crazy?
He's just a designer
As fine as his line
Watching him stitch every single time
It's his skills that get you
His smartness that makes you imagine
It's the machine you hear going
Not the table rocking
He's the designer

Inspired by a dear friend
Par Le Patreq the Designer

The Note

He had a passion

It wasn't just writing

Or scribbling anything on the paper

He spent hours and days making beats

His hands went across the keyboard in melody

He wasn't an average dude

He was a musical genius

And a producer like no other

He was creative

He put everything together

And became a dope rapper

Talent started to become his first name

Not the one given at birth when he came.

Day and night

Music was his life

On the train even at the bus stop

His mind spun like a ferris wheel

The internal parts of his body made him feel

That this roller coaster he's on was definitely real.

Gifted Hands

A pinch of salt, a dab of pepper, a sprinkle of Mrs.Dash
Lets mix it all together
Gifted hands starting at the age five
Helping grandma in the kitchen all the time
Choosing to stay in the house to learn all the ingredients
Instead of going outside to play hide and seek
Grandma always told you your hands are special,
You wait, watch and see what I tell you
Gifted hands is for certain people only
The miracles that you will be able to do
Don't forget what grandma told you
6 bars of 10oz cracker barrel cheese, eggs, carnation milk,
seasoning, salt & pepper
When you put it all together, this makes macaroni & cheese
One of the gifted hand's favorite dishes
It will melt in your mouth like a piece of candy
Grandma always told me my hands were gifted
Now I cater for a variety of people
Gifted hands is one of my best qualities

Inspired by a dear friend
Rashawna Brown aka Muffin

Barber Shop

When I think of barber shops

The first thing that comes to my mind

Is the guy code

It's a social place

Where anything goes

Its therapeutic

You sit in the barbers chair

As he starts to prepare

With the sharp edge clippers

The design

He's about to get busy

The conversations continue

About sports, news, and even freaky ladies

It's the barber shop

A social place

To let loose; to be uninhibited

The conversation stays in the shop,

not to be carried out

After hours of being there

Your barber has cleaned you up

Sprayed the liquid on your head

Now its time to shut up.

Old Friends

We were only teens when we first met
Damn look at us now
We are all grown up
It is strange how you catch up with old friends
You see them and say
What did I miss?
The thoughts about what is going on with the person
Seeing how great they look
Wondering if they're taken
Old friends is all we are
Remember those high school days
Trying to figure out
How did we allow each other to get so far?
Old friends is all we are
The exchange of phone numbers
Is it good or is it bad?
We both are trying to start something from the past
The lust the two of us always had
Is this good or is it bad?
Internally I feel gushy
My body is overwhelmed trying to process how I feel right now
Old friends is all we are
Sizing him up like a pair of pants
Not knowing what to expect from this man
I feel like a little kid
Smiling from ear to ear.
Oh...old friend

He Makes Me Go hmmm....

It was this guy
But he was different than the rest
He listened, gave good feed-back and was very mature
Surprisingly sweet
Although he was somewhat discreet
He helped me understand
How a man should treat a woman no matter what the
circumstances
This guy came right on time
Aside from his intellectual being
He was caring and fine as wine

It was this guy
He helped me to see my worth
He showed me to put what was important first
Although he wasn't any of my children's father
He developed a bond with them
A lot of times, men don't think this matter's
But when you become a grown man
You learn to handle things with care from every angle

It was this guy
He was very passionate with my feelings
He always thought before he spoke so I could understand him
He gave great advice on how to deal with situations
He always knew exactly what to say to me
He was like an angel who dropped down from heaven
He knew just how to handle me
I thank God till this day, for allowing such a man to come my
way

What a Smile

Brown skin, Chinky eyes
Damn it's been a while
Where have you been?
Where has the time gone?

You have a great sense of humor

The feeling I got
Sitting in a room with you real quiet
My inner soul
Want to burst

My thoughts are going crazy
I don't know if I should stay
Or rip my clothes off and go at it
The melodies are playing

You're singing to the rhythm
I'm freaking out
Talking to myself
Saying girl, you're bugging out

I'm watching you read my work
You look up at me
With this expression
What the fuck

What a Smile
I sit up and start dancing to the music
You get up and left the room

I'm feeling really sexy
I'm instantly turning into my seductive self

Now, I hear you in the shower washing up
Thoughts ran through my mind, if I should join you
The tunes are still playing
I stood tall

I started to wine to the music
Oh boy
My body was over heated
I was facing the window

You walked to the door
You stop, stood there
And started watching me
What a Smile!

Identity

It was something special about her
She had that look you would want
Brown skin with beautiful lips
Wide hips
She had a walk that was it
Her personality was passive, loving, caring and fun
She knew how to entertain anyone
When she walked the streets
People knew who she was
And would always speak

It was something special about her
She kept a smile on her face
She never gave signs of being disgraced
The confidence in her made her sexy in every way
She had a perky attitude everyday

It was something special about her
Whenever she was around
Her presence was felt
She gave off good energy in her aura
The sun appeared to always be out
She was forceful in a great way
She would inspire anyone I must say

It was something special about her
The high tolerance level
Some people tried to under-estimate her
Took her kindness for a weakness
She was so damn unique
Her words were so smooth
Any individual
If they had to choose without a doubt
It would be her

It was something special about her
She had a way about her
Well liked
She opened her doors
To help anyone out
She never judged
She welcomed people
Always made them feel comfortable
It was something special about her...

Fake Chicks

They smile up in your face

Act like your good friends

But in the end it was all a scheme

"Bitches"

That's what they are

Think I'm a fool

But yet they're giving off clues

You try to keep it real but that doesn't help

It's too much jealousy

Is it worth me putting myself to work

For what?

Fake chicks

Who want to be in my face

Wishing they had the things I have

Look the way I look

Confidence is what you call it

Not conceited, as they tried to perceive it

Strong female

A people's person too damn nice

Wake up and play their game

No, its not over it just started

I'm about to shut it down

And disregard those

"Bitches"

That's their name

I had to come out my character and play their way.

Words Can't Break Me

These dudes want to bring you down
They say hurtful things
To make you feel like a clown
Demeaning others to boost their self- esteem
Coward
Where are your balls?
You speak those words just to make me feel small
Is that the job of a man?
If it is, I don't want any part of it
I thought they were put on this earth
To protect women,
Nurture their souls and
Treat them like a princess
What's happened to this world today?
There are so many men out of place
It's like a puzzle needed put together
Dealing with a man for 11 and half years and going through a
struggle…
What happened to a man respecting his lady?
Don't try to under estimate who I am and try to play me
My creativeness is golden
This man always saying I'm not motivated
Whose time clock am I on?
Can I not work according to my timeline?
A man tries to decrease my value
If only he could admit, he sees my power.

Monkey see Monkey do

Who are you?

SCORN

You look at me

Like I'm the

ENEMY

Somewhere in your mind

You think not having a house

Will belittle me

Who are you?

I know who I am

BEAUTIFUL

You think your smart

But when I open my mouth

You act surprised

The

VENGEANCE

You express

ANGER

Because I stood up for myself

Who are you?

WICKED

You try to do things

That might affect me

REALLY!

You still don't know who I am

Strong Female

Who can get through any storm?

MISERABLE

The act of oneself displayed without any thought

Who are you?

PITIFUL

Your preventive methods to immature

To not understand why I'm over you

Monkey see

Monkey

Should not do

It makes life more difficult for you

And when you're done, you will see

How much you will lose

Who are you?

A Coward

Monkey see

Monkey should not do!

It Was A Thought!

She woke up one day
Her thought was to educate
That thought was put into motion
She came up with to promote and educate individuals about cancer

Diamond
She started Shades of a Cure
One of the best things anyone could have done
Today, its been years now since they have stomped out in pumps

Come out, check the internet and read about them
Shades of a Cure
They're here to teach the community
Don't be in denial in let this great information pass you by

Stay in tuned with the various events
Wine, Cheese and Gossip
Donate your bras day
Pick up a T-shirt "Hey cancer, you messed with the wrong bitch."

Inspired by a dear friend Diamond
Founder for " Shades of a Cure" Non-Profit Org.

Joy Survives

It was a dark moment
Diagnoses… cancer
Every nerve in her body
Deprived of sensation
Oblivious
SHOCKED
She cried
Where is my Joy
Hearing those words replaying over and over
CANCER
Her tear stained face
The phone calls she had to make
Stage 3
Now the performance of her life begins
She thought to herself
I am dead
Where is my Joy
Test after test
To kill the living cell
Feeling hopeless in her living hell
In fact it was just the beginning
The changes that she had to make
Her support system was on deck
Her spirit radiated from the chemo
A queen
Without her thick wool crown
Ejecting her soul
Liable to break
Feeling unclean
Echoes of strength
Renewed her belief and
The darkness became light
Her crown restored
There is my Joy

Inspired by Joy aka Juicy

High Roller

The ability to become so talented
Mastering something you love in with passion
Doing it over and over until you perfect it
I have never seen anyone like her
Yeah
Cheese is her name
At 9 months pregnant, she did her thing
she was sliding, gliding and even dropping to the floor
At her baby shower she put on a fantastic skating show

The ability to become so talented
Mastering something you love in with passion
Week after week she hit the skating floor
I have never seen anyone like her before
Yeah
I said her name is Cheese
A high roller, she's been skating since a baby
She's creative, she takes risk, she's immaculate and flawless,
She's those things and much, much more
A worldwide roller skater, an old school dancer
She's multi talented
She's someone you would not want to battle

The ability to become so talented
Mastering something you love in with passion
Her motivation can inspire you
That gaze and you wonder how you can do it too
She makes it look so easy
It takes great work to become an experienced skater

Inspired by Cheese the Roller Skater

She Got It

Fabulous

That what you say

When you meet this lady from

Brooklyn

Startled

By the way

Those shoes maneuver your legs

The vibe a woman gives off

While she's working the crosswalk

It's always interesting to know

How she does it

High heels…how high

She sashays floating on air

That says a lot about

Jataime shoe wear

The fit, the size and style is tight

She has people coming from all over

to buy shoes for their left and their right

You might wonder

Why her clientele is up

But when you visit her store

That question is no longer a thought

The variety of shoes from which you can choose

I guarantee you won't come out with just one

She's in business for a reason

Foundations for all seasons

After your experience there

Step in before you step out

Because the soul is what she's all about!

Inspired by Jetaime Shoes

FACELESS

They watch
They stare
They wonder how she's there
High Maintenance Salon
Rocking every style in Christian Louboutins
She's the bomb
It's not just the strut in her walk
Or the fat in her butt
It could be you're envious
She's just a wise individual
A homeowner
A broker
An entrepreneur
Whose confidence is huge
She goes hard at everything she does
Truth be told
She's someone, you wish you was
Is she supposed to dumb herself down
Why?
To make them feel like they're on her level
Absolutely not!
She's to continue to give life all she's got!

Inspired by High Maintenance Salon

Oh Yeah!

Gorgeous nails she has
I sat, saw and wondered where she went
Who was the person who did them?
She appeared to be so flamboyant

The colors were just right
The design was hot
The shape... stiletto
Boy, I just had to know

She was eccentric
So I inquired
Who did your nails?
Vaguely she responded "an uptown girl"

Intrigued
I wanted to know more
"Salon, what is your name?"
I already know nails are your thing

"Oh really," I said
Tell me more
I'd like to visit
Beauty is a woman's decision

It will be a day well spent
The service there is excellent
All polished and sizzling
Now nails are my thing!

LADIES NIGHT

Let's get together for a girls night out
Always remember what Lafemme Suite is about
Fun, fun and more fun
Everyone is invited to come
Movement is how we get you
Moments like this, you won't want to miss
Every time you come for pole lessons or fun

Someone is always here who has patience
Unrevealed what you have learned
It adds a different spin for that special friend
Throw up your pole and turn on the tunes
Even your partner will be amused

Inspired by Lefemme Suite

Its Party Time

He started jumping around to the sound of the beat
I almost mistook him for Mohammad Ali
Because of the way he moved his feet
Every time the beat dropped
His spirit allowed him to pop right back up
It was that DJ
His music selection was crazy
3 promoters
Came together and made sure
This would be a night to remember
He was out there
On the dance floor
Do you remember White Chicks?
I almost mistook him for
Terry Cruz
Boy was he wasted
The way he was showing out
I was sure someone dropped a
Mickey in his drink
What this all came down to
It was that DJ's music
He knew exactly what to do
That party was rocking
Everyone was on the dance floor sweaty and hot
Now, that's how a DJ
Is supposed to spin those records

The Dribble

Draft pick

He's on his game

Now a jersey wears his name

It wasn't about how long he played

It was the fact that he made it

The GOD

Went from street ball

To the big lights

His skills were impeccable

And he was going to rock

Known for his dribble

The boy couldn't be stopped

Three words to describe him

Strengths, speed and talent

Anyone could not have done this

Even after being injured

Nothing could stop him

A China import

Yao Ming

MVP'S

That has to tell you something

About the man he is

The GOD

Even Reebok and Converse bowed at his feet

Word

This guy is no joke

Divine Providence

Coach

Trainer

Mentor

The GOD of the dribble

Inspired by a dear friend God Shammgod

Draft pick to the NBA in 1997

COCOLITA

Cocolita

Is what her family calls her

Why?

She has a Spanish mother and a black father

Cocolita was something special

Being on her own since 16 wasn't easy

The trails and tribulations she has gone through

Suffering from domestic violence with this dude

Her journey was just starting

Once she finally departed the life that caused her pain

She stepped into a new arena where she could use her talent

Music became Cocolita's world

She went from little jobs to managing everything

Today she is a General Manager for CTE

Her skills are like no other

She's very detailed with her work

Even with the artists

It's the smallest things she knows

What kind of candy do you like?

Your type of drink?

Her entire style down to your feet

Cocolita has her days

Of course

She's overworked

Lack of sleep

A caring mother

A leader

But

She's DOPE

A dependable person

Anyone would love

to have her on their team

she's far from mean and you will be pleased

Inspired by my dear friend Erica Bowen

General Manager of Corporate Thug Ent.

"1993"

Russ is known for his Barber shop

I bet you didn't know he owns half the block

"1993" the birth of his business

Wait, stop, look

He is every bit of a gentleman

When you sit in his chair you'll feel right at home

It's not a hangout but he'll hook up your dome

A professional place

No drinking allowed

A place to visit

A place for the proud

If you happen to have your wife with you

Big Russ Hair salon will hook up her do

Everything is done there

Wash and sets, weaves, color and cuts

Russ spots

Yup

They're what's up

Whenever you're in Harlem

Just stop by

Get your hair did and be Big Russ fly!

Inspired by Big Russ Barber Shop

JUST WEAR IT

Wolfstyle clothing is must have gear

Obviously the items there are dope wear

Lots of different styles to select from

Flossing just shirts is not their only one

Spitting lyrics on mix tapes are something else they do great

Tell a friend to tell a friend to stop in there

Location is easy, just hop on the train

Yes its worth the visit

Either way your time there will be splendid

Inpired by Wolfstyle

Footsteps

I found out
I was having a girl
I shopped everywhere
For bows to put in her hair
Frustrated
By not having any luck
A plan was needed
To start my own boutique
You Me and Dupri came about
A kids clothing boutique
NICE
That's what I had to do without a doubt
I knew anything I ordered would sell out
This was just the beginning of my journey
It wasn't only about my appearance
I needed brains behind my madness
I took classes to enhance this
Let me not take all the credit
There was a contractor building my dream
Now, when you walk in my boutique
It's full of love, colors and happiness
You Me and Dupri is the children's place to be
Clothing is not our only specialty
I celebrate birthdays and always have special invited guests
So when you're thinking of something to do
Don't hesitate to look me up

Inspired by You Me and Dupri

It Works

There I stood

Looking in the mirror

What I saw was my reflection

Unhappy

Every time I looked at myself

I became real angry

The thought was in my head

How I would change this

The physical part of me was not ready to do it

Year after year went by

Every summer I said I would try

A friend of mine introduced me to Herbalife

The first thing that came to mind was yuk

My immature being

Only to find out Herbalife was something healthy

It helps with weight –management and personal care

I took some time to understand all of this

Today millions of people are doing it

The location in Harlem on 135ᵗʰ even offers aerobics

So, before you decide to put up a fight

Take some time to learn about Herbalife

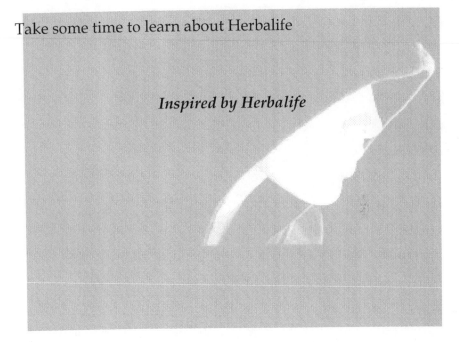

Inspired by Herbalife

HARLEM BOYZ

Vroom Vroom

Is what you hear coming down 8th ave

Those Harlem Boyz are something else

When they come its never just one

Bikers from different boroughs and states are riding

It's like a windy day when they're around

Everyone on the sidewalk appears to be moving slow

All the while those bikes are passing by just putting on a show

It's one biker in particular

He's known by the name

Superman

Fly, fly, and fly away

You better watch out

And that's all I'm going to say

Vroom Vroom

Is the sound of their bikes

But let's be clear

That's not all they're about

They are great role models who know how to unite

They support many positive things throughout New York

So when you see them riding down your street

Throw up a peace sign and let them be

Inspired by my friend Will aka Superman

Harlem Boyz

SOULFOOD

Something so very tasteful, Amy Ruth

    The place people love to eat

Okra is known to be a southern dish

    Macaroni & Cheese, Salmon Croquetts and Baked Catfish

    has a tasteful bliss

Underneath the mind of a soulfood cooker

    comes creative ideas about how to prepare them

Lord have mercy you have to taste it

    Those Smothered Porkchops, Turkey Wings and Collard

    Greens

For sure you will be pleased

    The Meat Loaf, Sautéed Chicken Liver, Spare Ribs and Grilled

    Strip Steak

Other than all that good food

    Amy Ruth has a nice ambiance

Outstanding customer service

Don't ever say you can't find a southern food restaurant because Amy

    Ruth's has it.

Inspired by Amy Ruth's

The Series

You might watch it in the living room
You might watch it in the family room
You may even go into the bedroom
Who knows you might stand in the kitchen

Check it out
Check it out
This new sexy soap opera style drama
Everyone is talking about it

It's about three male best friends
They are all dating
Their friendship gets messy
But they all have professional careers

Lenox Avenue, A Sexy Dramatic Series in Harlem
It's New
Something that's going to put a spin on Television
It's different
It's a diversity of characters showing off their talents

Lenox Avenue, A Sexy Dramatic Series
A Program created by actor/producer Al Thompson

Diversity

Have you ever been to a place?
And when you looked around
There was so much diversity
The environment was not just a scene of
Different skin colors
It was a multitude of
Business owners,
Entrepreneurs,
Skilled individuals
That came out
To socialize, drink, eat and network
The Corner Social
Is at a convenient location
A place filled with
Good people, music and laughter
Conversations held there are ever lasting
It's almost like you're having a dream
Something replaying in your mind
Once you make a visit there
The Corner Social will become a part of your daily living

Inspired by Corner Social

Chill Berry

You're very cold to me

At times you could be real;

Slimy, crunchy, soft, sweet, chewy

You make me have a brain freeze

That sharp pain going through my head

I have to close my eyes to wait for it to go away

Ummm. The thought of such good taste

It's hard all around but very smooth and silky in the middle

The circular movement as its coming out

It always looks just right

There are so many to choose from

It is so overwhelming that I cannot pick one

All of those beautiful colors!

Inspired by HARLEMYO Est.

Event Planners

For a job well done, amazed by the outcome.
Although they could not visualize it, they loved every bit.
The imagination of their thoughts, Lambert Treasures were chosen.
Excited by what they saw, the room was the best fit.

Although they could not visualize it, they loved every bit.
Anxious to see all the details, the ones they requested.
Excited by what they saw, the room was the best fit.
What was presented, were Lambert Treasures creative reflections.

Anxious to see all the details, the ones they requested.
The fairytale they longed for, their dreams were coming true.
What was presented, were Lambert Treasures creative reflections.
Their days were numbered, oh how their enthusiasm grew.

The fairytale they longed for, their dreams were coming true.
Not knowing were to start, they pondered on what to do.
Their days were numbered, oh how their enthusiasm grew.
They researched and made phone calls, they had no clue.

Not knowing were to start, they pondered on what to do.
Lambert Treasures saved them, their work is impeccable.
They researched and made phone calls, they had no clue.
The day was finally here, the room was beautiful.

Inspired by Lambert Treasure

Hard Work

Courage, Beliefs, Strengths
You make every second, minute and hour count
You use your time wisely to get what you want
It takes great discipline to stay focused on what you would
like to accomplish
Not being at every party;
Leave that to the promoters
Wants are things you could live without
Needs are things you must have without a doubt
Some individuals make light of what you are about
A hard worker is someone who put time in.
Whatever that job may be
If you put your all into it, you could shine like me
As Booker T. Washington said;
"Success is measured not so much by the position reached in
life as by the obstacles overcome while trying to succeed"
Hard work leads into many things
You're able to save money, spend good times with friends
and family.
Hard work is not a joke.

Inspired by
My friends Melicia and Dameeka

ACKNOWLEDGEMENTS

Jetaime Shoes
198 Flatbush Avenue
Brooklyn, NY 11217
347-799-1458

Garden State Plaza Mall
Paramus, NJ 07652
201-845-Shoe

High Maintenance Salon
2244 7th Avenue
New York, NY 10027

Lafemme Suite
2364 Adam Clayton Powell Jr Blvd
New York, NY 10030

Big Russ
2470A 8th Avenue
New York, NY 10027

Wolfstyle
2470 B Fredrick Douglas BLVD
New York, NY 10027
212-926-WOLF

You Me and Dupri
2297 7th Avenue,
New York, NY 10035

Herbalife
201 West 135th Street
New York, NY 10030

Corner Social
321 Lenox Avenue
New York, NY 10027

Inspired by HARLEMYO Est.
2121 Fredrick Douglas BLVD
New York, NY 10027

Amy Ruth's
113 W 116th Street
New York, NY 10026

Lambert Treasures
2916 Frederick Douglas BLVD, Unit 3A
New York, NY 10039
212-926-9822

27277776R00071

Made in the USA
Charleston, SC
04 March 2014